THE GENOME OF THE FAITH

OF THE FAITH

A Life Unfolding Between Heaven and Earth

A Scientist's
Testament
Beyond The
Timeline

GOLD SEAL OF EXCELLENCE
★★★★★
ARPRESS
TOP-RATED BOOK

Dr. Ulysses Labilles

ARPress

ARPress
45 Dan Road Suite 5
Canton MA 02021
Hotline: 1(888) 821-0229
Fax: 1(508) 545-7580

Ordering Information:
Quantity sales. Special discounts are available on quantity purchases by corporations, associations, and others. For details, contact the publisher at the address above.

Printed in the United States of America.

ISBN-13:   Softcover   979-8-89676-417-5
                  eBook   979-8-89676-418-2

Library of Congress Control Number: 2025909757

Table of Contents

Dedication

You have been my light and heartbeat to Reighben,
Duanne, Dwight, and Abby. To my family, by blood
and faith, united in purpose, courage, and compassion,
may you always walk with love, lead with integrity, and live with grace.
Dedicated to those fighting illness.
Your Story matters, and you are never alone. I also
Dedicate this book to the patients I served as a dental
medicine clinician and the lives I touched as a COVID-19
Response Corps epidemiologist with the CDC Foundation.

Preface

Writing this book serves to share my journey from my roots to my battle with cancer and to test my cognitive load after two craniotomies. As an epidemiologist, I believed science had solutions to every problem through asking the right questions, collecting data, and analyzing. This guided me through research, public health crises, and the COVID-19 pandemic. However, life's complexity reveals questions beyond science's scope. Following a diagnosis of stage 4 non-small cell lung cancer with brain metastasis, and subsequent brain surgery to address a lesion that caused a midline shift, my perspective on illness and recovery changed significantly. I went from observer to patient, healer to need healing, gaining insight beyond science. This book combines science and faith, detailing my health journey and spiritual growth. It shows how science enhanced my appreciation of everyday moments and how grace, an unearned favor providing strength and peace, taught me about life's fragility and the power of surrendering to God.

The diagnosis of stage 4 cancer is a harrowing experience, one that shakes the very foundations of life and challenges every belief and hope. As an epidemiologist, I have spent years studying patterns, causes, and effects of health and disease conditions in defined populations. Yet, nothing could prepare me for the personal battle I would face with cancer. This is a chronicle of my journey, the promising future of precision oncology, and the divine strength and peace I found in grace. Each chapter offers experiences from medical procedures, chemotherapy, solitude, prayer, and love, providing insights into facing mortality and blending science with belief. In the depths of despair, after receiving the diagnosis, I found myself grappling with the reality of my condition. The statistics were grim, and the prognosis was daunting. Stage 4 cancer, often referred to as metastatic cancer, signifies that the disease has spread to distant parts of the body. It is a battle fought on many fronts—physical, emotional, and spiritual. The treatments were intense. Chemotherapy, radiation, and experimental therapies became my new regular. Each day was a struggle, marked by pain, fatigue, and the ever-present shadow of uncertainty. I am deeply grateful for the support and love from my family, friends, and the medical community. Your dedication and expertise have been a beacon of hope in my darkest hours. I have included an 'Acknowledgments' section in this book to express my gratitude.

Yet, amidst the turmoil, I found moments of reflection and resilience. The lens through which I viewed my life began to shift. What had once been a purely scientific pursuit became intertwined with a profound spiritual awakening. While pursuing science and medicine, I discovered faith. Grace, an unearned favor providing strength and peace, became central to my journey. Based on personal experiences rather than scientific evidence, grace appeared during difficult times, offering strength as a gift—a testament to faith and a higher power. During cancer treatment, I found peace, alleviating fears and anxieties. Prayer, meditation, and my relationship with God brought solace. As an epidemiologist, I valued scientific knowledge but saw the harmony between science and grace, which is integral to life and healing. This book stresses the importance of blending science and faith, enlightening the reader and encouraging an open-minded approach to healing. My resilience in facing mortality, a testament to the human spirit's ability to overcome even the most daunting challenges, is a story of inspiration and empowerment. This book is a testament to that resilience, and I hope it inspires you, the reader, to find your strength in the face of adversity.

My journey began with exploring my identity. The surname Labilles is uncommon, tracing back to French expeditions in the Philippines. Labilles may be derived from Labille, French painter Adélaïde Labille Guiard, an early female member of the Royal Academy who advocated for women's education rights; Daniel Labille, Auxiliary Bishop of Soissons and Titular Bishop of Fata from 1978 to 1984, who became the Bishop of Soissons until 1998; and Belgian public servant Jean-Pascal Labille are among the Notable figures named Labille. While unrelated, I take pride in the legacy. As a Labilles, I contributed to public health during a pandemic, published research, and advocated for cancer awareness. My mother's maiden name, Lágrimas, means "tears" in Spanish and symbolizes devotion to Our Lady of Sorrows—a name likely adopted due to the Clavería Decree of 1849. Named after Ulysses S. Grant, I've gained historical insights and through his historical imprint, I've been led to emphasize endurance and grace. My heritage, a unique blend of European and Filipino cultures, has significantly shaped my identity and influenced my approach to cancer care, adding a personal touch to my journey. For instance, I remember the first time I saw a tulip in the garden of my childhood home, and it whispered hope to me. This memory has always been a source of strength for me, especially during the pandemic and my battle with cancer.

To my children, patients, and readers: This book is about my journey and your role. It addresses our challenges, acknowledges those who came before us, and celebrates the grace we've found. It is intended for those seeking knowledge about healing or maintaining faith while dealing with uncertainty. It suggests that questions are inherent, and that peace comes from trust rather than complete knowledge. Trust, a key message of this book, can provide comfort and guidance to those dealing with uncertainty—trust in the process, the support system, and the resilience of the human spirit. My journey has been guided by trust in the medical process, in the support of my loved ones, and the strength of the human spirit. This book discusses the concepts of trust and grace in overcoming life's challenges, highlighting their importance in offering reassurance during difficult times. The aim is to demonstrate that trust can be a valuable resource for all individuals. To those involved in the CDC Foundation COVID Response Corps and my research readers, this book serves as my contribution, rather than a farewell. I journeyed through sunny Southern California with my cousins Junjun and Olly, nieces Alyssa Jessamyn and Jaden, and nephew Asher. Each mile passed, and the breeze carried a sense of home. I have found my place of rest, not only on the earth but also in peace. Forest Lawn Covina Hills awaits my body, and God awaits my soul.

Psalm 62:5 (RSV): "For God alone my soul waits in silence; for my hope is from him."

Letter to the Readers

Dear Beloved Readers:

Before you turn the next page, thank you for reading my story and letting it be part of your journey. These pages include scientific data, diagnoses, and observations. You'll find detailed records of CT scans, MRIs, and surgeries. You will also come across individuals I've known, those who have passed away, and those whose impact endures over time and distance, their memories living on in the pages of this book.

I share my story not to highlight my resilience but to demonstrate the support I have received. This support has enabled me to surpass any diagnosis. I did not write this book because I had all the answers. I wrote it because I encountered the questions that many of us face when dealing with illness, grief, or transition. Questions about the future, the meaning of life, and the balance between science and faith. If you are facing challenges, know that you are not alone. We may walk different paths but share a common journey, and the guiding light is the same. I hope my story encourages, not as a testament to personal strength, but as an example of perseverance beyond any prognosis. With all my love and Care,

Dr. Ulysses Lagrimas Labilles

Petals of Grace, Shadows of Silent Wars: Where the Light Touched the Wound

Even in the quietest bloom

As I could hear the whispers of the Easter tulips, I suddenly reminisced on silent wars I've known. Through sterile halls where charts were hung, I could hear the echoes of remembered pains with each footstep down the St. Louis University campus. Even in the quietest bloom, grace appears alongside grief. In places where conflict occurs quietly, peace emerges in small ways. "The Lord will fight for you; you must only be still." Exodus 14:14 (RSV) I wandered through life's memories, lost breaths, forgotten clinical notes, nights without hope. Yet Easter bloomed in tulip grace, Bright hymns of color in every place. The petals of the Easter tulips were in the sunlight, and I went to the open church. St. Francis Xavier, with doors open wide, A whispered prayer, a softened soul, always in a silent war, my heart beating slowly, concerns, ushers while tulip blooms sing, even silent wars, from the pandemic to my battle with cancer, can find a room. I stood as a sentinel behind unseen walls amid daily virtual meetings, midnight calls, and emails. I was a silent soldier in a war of breath, on a battlefield where science met a thousand deaths. The world was chaos, masked and blurred, each case a name, each name a word. I traced the arcs, rates, and spread while holding back my private dread. Even as I charted fate, my own would knock, unasked, irate. A shadow in my lung took hold, A story that refused the mold. Cancer came without remorse, A silent storm that changed my course. Not just a cell, but fate's cruel thief, that tested love, faith, and grief. But of all the fears that filled my night, not pain, loss, nor even fight, it was the sharp and near thought of leaving without those I hold dear.

To slip away and not have said, I love you," before the final thread. Missing the touch of familiar hands and the sound of my name called one last time. Yet every day, I find the light in voices soft, in love's invite. In those who stayed, who fought, who wept, who whispered strength while others slept. I write to heal, but to remember, breathe, and feel. That though I battled in the dark, Love lit each step, each silent mark. My connection to the pandemic and cancer is a reminder of the shared human experience and the need for empathy and understanding.

In 2020, the world stood still, but alarms were ringing for public health workers. It felt like a war without uniforms or borders, fought not with weapons but with data, discipline, and prayer. As an epidemiologist, I learned to analyze transmission patterns, viral mutations, and risk factors. I studied the language of illness and believed that understanding science could lead to saving lives. And we did, but there were days when science alone was insufficient. When COVID-19 surged through the Navajo Nation, I realized that love, presence, and grace mattered just as much. The Navajo Nation, with its rich cultural heritage and deep spiritual ties to the land, has long struggled with systemic poverty, limited access to healthcare, and entrenched health disparities.

The pandemic magnified those inequalities. Many homes lacked clean, running water, and people lived far from the nearest clinics or hospitals. I worked alongside a team of dedicated public health professionals, tribal leaders, and volunteers to manage care, allocate resources, and support those most affected. We did our best to treat patients, track outbreaks, and reduce harm, but healing required more than data: compassion. Science helped me understand the virus, but grace helped me understand the people. During the pandemic, I experienced severe fatigue, headaches, dizziness, and shortness of breath. The United States Department of Veterans Affairs reviewed my professional experience at the CDC Foundation. The Research and Development Service at the VA St. Louis extended an offer for me to join the clinical Epidemiology team. My lecture series on long COVID has gained international attention, leading me to a new role at VA Long Beach as a research affiliate and federal contractor for the Southern California Institute for Research and Education. On November 2, 2023, during onboarding,

I was admitted to Barnes-Jewish Center Neuro ICU. Born Hiram Ulysses Grant, who later became the 18th President of the United States, and after whom I am named, exemplifies courage, leadership, and resilience.

Reflecting on my journey, I find a deep connection that transcends time and circumstance with a historical figure. His unwavering resolve and dignified approach to life's battles inspire me to lead with purpose and face my challenges with fortitude. As I navigate my final war, my battle with stage 4 cancer is formidable, but it is also a journey of transformation. Advances in precision oncology offer hope for improved survival and quality of life. The science of grace provides strength and peace that sustains and uplifts. As an epidemiologist and a person of faith, I have embraced my journey's scientific and spiritual dimensions. In science, I sought answers; through grace, I found strength and peace. May this account serve as a testament to the resilience of the human spirit and the boundless possibilities that arise when science and faith converge. Reminding me that authentic leadership is defined by the battles we fight and the grace with which we face them. While Grant faced his final war with dignity, battling illness with the same resolve and clarity that defined his military career.

In a poignant parallel, I am now facing my final war as a stage 4 cancer patient. I confront this challenge with dignity, purpose, and clarity, and the example of his facing adversity with grace continues to guide me. After the craniotomy procedure to remove a metastasis on the right side of the brain, I began receiving a precision oncology treatment plan following the diagnosis of stage 4 non-small cell lung cancer adenocarcinoma subtype. The primary lesion was in the lung, while the tumor removed from the brain was secondary. Precision oncology, a beacon of hope, utilizes advanced genomic sequencing technologies to identify genetic alterations and biomarkers driving tumor growth and progression. Through a deeper understanding of the molecular mechanisms underlying cancer, targeted therapies have been developed to inhibit or disrupt these aberrant pathways selectively. This individualized approach has shown remarkable efficacy in improving survival rates by providing me with treatments that directly address the unique characteristics of their tumors.

Moreover, precision oncology has not only contributed to enhancing my quality of life as a cancer patient but has also transformed it. By minimizing unnecessary toxicities and side effects associated with traditional chemotherapy, targeted therapies reduce the burden on patients' physical and emotional well-being. Additionally, the ability to predict treatment responses and potential toxicities through genomic profiling allows for proactive management and personalized supportive care, further improving patients' quality of life. The transformative impact of precision oncology on cancer care has set the stage for the potential recognition of Nobel Prize-worthy achievements. The development and implementation of targeted therapies have revolutionized the treatment landscape, offering hope to untreatable patients. The precision oncology field continues to evolve rapidly, with ongoing research focused on discovering novel genetic targets and improving therapeutic strategies, advancing the likelihood of future Nobel-worthy breakthroughs. Precision oncology could significantly improve cancer patients' survival rates and quality of life by leveraging genetic insights to develop targeted therapies.

The potential for Nobel recognition stems from the groundbreaking advancements in understanding and treating cancer at the molecular level. From extensive cancer-specific genomic sequencing to using artificial intelligence to develop cancer vaccines, precision oncology continues to evolve; its potential for further transformative achievements in cancer care remains high, inspiring hope for the future of cancer treatment and recognition on a prestigious global stage. While undergoing various diagnostic imaging tests, treatments, and surgeries, I found that the scientific methods I supported were instrumental in my treatment. Through procedures such as craniotomy, radiation therapy, and tumor profiling, a genetic mutation (MET exon 14) was identified, making me eligible for targeted therapy. Precision oncology aims to match treatment to a tumor's specific genetic characteristics. The current medical landscape is marked by an ongoing battle to improve survival rates for various conditions and diseases, with one of the most formidable challenges being the treatment of cancer. Despite significant progress in cancer research and treatment options, the complexity and heterogeneity of tumors have made it challenging to achieve optimal outcomes for patients.

This necessitates exploring innovative solutions and advancements in medical technology to address these challenges effectively. One such solution that holds immense promise is precision oncology. Provide specific details about the prevalence and impact of cancer, highlighting the need for improved survival rates. Discuss the limitations of current treatment approaches and the potential of precision oncology to revolutionize cancer care.

Cancer continues to be a leading cause of death worldwide, with millions of lives affected by this devastating disease. Despite advancements in chemotherapy, radiation therapy, and surgery, the overall survival rates for certain types of cancer remain low. This is primarily due to the heterogeneity of tumors, which makes it challenging to develop targeted treatments that effectively eradicate cancer cells while minimizing harm to healthy tissues. Precision oncology, however, offers a paradigm shift by leveraging advanced technologies and genetic profiling to tailor treatments to individual patients based on their unique molecular characteristics. The challenges' implications are limited treatment options, adverse side effects, and suboptimal outcomes.

Emphasize the urgency and significance of finding effective interventions to improve survival rates and enhance the quality of life for cancer patients.
The limitations of current treatment approaches in oncology highlight the urgent need for innovative solutions. Conventional therapies often result in systemic toxicity, compromising the overall well-being of patients. Furthermore, the lack of treatment options for specific subsets of cancer patients, such as those with rare mutations or drug-resistant tumors, underscores the necessity for advancements in medical technology. Precision oncology offers the potential to address these challenges by enabling personalized therapies tailored to the specific genetic alterations driving the growth and spread of tumors. Pursuing

advancements in medical technology, specifically precision oncology, is vital to transform cancer care and improve patient outcomes. Discuss how embracing this innovative approach aligns with any organization's mission and vision. By embracing precision oncology, healthcare organizations can position themselves at the forefront of cancer care, providing patients with cutting-edge treatments with the highest chance of success. Advanced technologies such as next-generation sequencing and molecular profiling allow healthcare professionals to detect genetic alterations and provide patients with suitable therapies.

This approach not only improves survival rates but also minimizes unnecessary treatments and reduces the burden on patients, both physically and emotionally. In summary, precision oncology holds immense promise in revolutionizing cancer care. Precision oncology can improve treatment outcomes, enhance patient quality of life, optimize healthcare resources, and advance cancer research by analyzing a tumor's genetic profile and tailoring treatments accordingly. Embracing this innovative approach can significantly impact the medical landscape, bringing us one step closer to finding effective interventions and improving survival rates for cancer patients. Precision oncology, also known as personalized or targeted therapy, is a revolutionary approach to cancer treatment that aims to tailor medical interventions to the specific genetic and molecular characteristics of an individual's tumor. Unlike conventional medicines, which often take a one-size-fits-all approach, precision oncology recognizes that each patient's cancer is unique and requires a customized treatment plan. At the heart of precision oncology is analyzing a tumor's genetic profile through techniques such as next-generation sequencing. By identifying specific genetic alterations, oncologists can gain crucial insights into the driving mechanisms behind the tumor's growth and spread.

This allows them to select targeted therapies that act directly on these alterations, inhibiting the tumor's progression. One of the primary benefits of precision oncology is its potential to improve treatment outcomes. By tailoring therapies to match the genetic characteristics of a tumor, precision oncology can increase the efficacy of treatment while minimizing the risk of adverse side effects. This is particularly significant for patients with rare mutations or drug-resistant tumors who may have limited treatment options using traditional approaches. Precision oncology provides them with new possibilities for effective treatment. Additionally, precision oncology has the potential to enhance patient quality of life. Conventional treatments often involve systemic therapies that can cause significant toxicity and negatively impact patients' overall well-being. With precision oncology, targeted therapies can spare healthy cells and tissues, reducing the severity and frequency of side effects. This allows patients to maintain a higher quality of life during their treatment journey. Another advantage of precision oncology is its ability to identify patients who are most likely to benefit from specific treatments. By analyzing a tumor's genetic makeup, oncologists can determine which patients are more likely to respond positively to a particular therapy, thus avoiding unnecessary treatments for those unlikely to benefit. This approach improves patient outcomes and optimizes healthcare resources by focusing on the most effective interventions. Furthermore, precision oncology has the potential to drive advancements in cancer research. By collecting and analyzing genomic data from patients undergoing precision oncology treatments, researchers can gain valuable insights into the underlying mechanisms of various cancers. This knowledge can lead to developing new targeted therapies and discovering biomarkers to aid in early detection and prognosis. Precision oncology holds immense promise in revolutionizing cancer care. Precision oncology can improve treatment outcomes, enhance patient quality of life, optimize healthcare resources, and advance cancer research by analyzing a tumor's genetic profile and tailoring treatments accordingly. Embracing this innovative approach can significantly impact the medical landscape, bringing us one step closer to finding effective interventions and improving cancer patients' survival rates. It is a revolutionary approach to cancer treatment that aims to tailor medical interventions to the specific genetic and molecular characteristics of an individual's tumor. Unlike conventional medicines, which often take a one-size-fits-all approach, precision oncology recognizes that each patient's cancer is unique and requires a customized treatment plan.

At the heart of precision oncology is analyzing a tumor's genetic profile through techniques such as next-generation sequencing. By identifying specific genetic alterations, oncologists can gain crucial insights into the driving mechanisms behind the tumor's growth and spread. This allows them to select targeted therapies that act directly on these alterations, inhibiting the tumor's progression. One of the primary benefits of precision oncology is its potential to improve treatment outcomes. By tailoring therapies to match the genetic characteristics of a tumor, precision oncology can increase the efficacy of treatment while minimizing the risk of adverse side effects. This is particularly significant for patients with rare mutations or drug-resistant tumors who may have limited treatment options using traditional approaches. Precision oncology provides them with new possibilities for effective treatment. Precision oncology can improve patient quality of life by using targeted therapies that reduce side effects compared to conventional systemic treatments. Analyzing a tumor's genetics identifies patients who will benefit from specific treatments, avoiding unnecessary ones for others.

This approach improves patient outcomes and optimizes healthcare resources by focusing on the most effective interventions. Moreover, precision oncology has the potential to drive advancements in cancer research. By collecting and analyzing genomic data from patients undergoing precision oncology treatments, researchers can gain valuable insights into the underlying mechanisms of various cancers. This knowledge can lead to developing new targeted therapies and discovering biomarkers to aid in early detection and prognosis. Precision oncology represents a beacon of hope for cancer patients. It is an innovative approach to cancer treatment that considers individual variability in genes, environment, and lifestyle. Precision oncology customizes treatment based on the genetic profile of a patient's cancer, improving effectiveness and reducing side effects. Through genetic profiling, oncologists can identify specific mutations and alterations in cancer cells. This information helps create therapies that target cancer cells and avoid healthy tissues. These therapies have shown remarkable success in improving overall survival rates and enhancing the quality of life for patients. Another promising frontier in precision oncology is immunotherapy. This treatment harnesses the power of the patient's immune system to fight cancer. By stimulating the body's natural defenses, immunotherapy offers a more personalized and less invasive approach to cancer care. Clinical trials and ongoing research continue to expand our understanding and application of these innovative treatments. Integrating artificial intelligence (AI) and big data analytics in precision oncology is changing cancer care. AI algorithms can analyze large amounts of data to identify patterns and predict outcomes, helping oncologists make informed and timely decisions. This data-driven approach improves the accuracy of treatment plans and provides patients with adequate care. Immunotherapy is a significant development in precision oncology, which uses the patient's immune system to combat cancer. Immunotherapy stimulates the body's natural defenses and offers a personalized and less invasive method of treating cancer. Clinical trials and ongoing research continue to expand knowledge and application of these treatments.

Gathered in Grace: A Community Experience

Prayer fosters family unity and compassion. It's a lifeline that connects us through distance, illness, and time. A family rooted in prayer can guide others through their challenges. My immediate family has provided substantial support, consistently believing in my aspirations even when I lacked confidence. Migration meant carrying home with me through faith, silence, and strength. I brought God into every room where my family prayed, cried, and hoped. They provided support during times of grief, illness, and Stage IV cancer with a silent strength that was reminiscent of my parents'. Matthew 18:20 states, "For where two or three gather in my name, there am I in the midst of them." This verse reminds me that true community isn't measured by numbers but by presence, specifically, God's presence. My first community was not a church or research team, but my family. My father was my coach, my mentor, and my first teacher. He instilled in me the discipline of tennis, waking me before dawn to run alongside him, our footsteps echoing our shared purpose. My mother demonstrated her love not through grand gestures but through the quiet consistency of her care, cooking, warmth, and ensuring

I was nourished after practice. Their passion was gentle but unwavering. When I left the Philippines, I carried their faith with me. Leaving the Philippines was not a decision made lightly. It was a crossroads shaped by duty as the eldest son, illness, and a fragile hope for something better. My father had suffered a stroke, and though he had always dreamed of retiring in the United States, his second stroke prevented him from making that journey. I went ahead with one foot in grief and the other in resolve, carrying the weight of his unrealized plans. I was a dentist with a practice and a family. Migration involves leaving behind routine, reputation, and familiarity. Arriving in America felt like starting fresh. During the uncertainty, I studied public health to explore more significant questions. Graduate school was a refuge and a test to remain faithful to God, and I never questioned the challenges that came upon me. I walked into St. Patrick Parish Church, not looking for answers but for stillness. I felt the quiet pulse of grace among strangers who gradually became companions.

I immersed myself in epidemiology, studying health and disease patterns, causes, and effects.

If I could not heal my family, perhaps I could help heal communities, and that belief kept me going. However, with every data set I analyzed and every health disparity I documented, I began to see what numbers could not explain: resilience, forgiveness, and unearned favor. Grace. I learned that life is about surrender, not control. The true calling lies in humbly receiving rather than measuring. At St. Patrick and St. Francis Xavier College Church, I realized faith goes beyond pews; it thrives in songs, Eucharist, and prayers of the sick and hopeful. Though I sought certainty in science, I found community in faith, struggling with doubt, grief, and failure. Yet, I also loved it. This realization, that faith is a source of resilience and hope, has been a guiding light in my journey, inspiring me to keep going even in the face of uncertainty.

The world began to speak a new language: lockdowns, surges, flattening curves, and personal protective equipment. For many, the pandemic was an unexpected event. For me, it arrived like a call to arms. As an epidemiologist, this was the moment I had dedicated my career to preparing for. No preparation could have prepared us for what happened. I had spent years analyzing data, building models, and teaching public health responses. Yet, the COVID-19 pandemic was not a theoretical exercise but a human catastrophe. Each number on a dashboard represented someone's father, sister, patient, or friend.

The work became intensely personal. I was no longer studying outbreaks; I was living through them. Days blurred into nights as the lines between science, policy, and morality grew fuzzy. We guided leaders, addressed misinformation, and analyzed the virus's development. Amidst it all, I start my day with a prayer. "O Lord. I am at the beginning of another day. I am uncertain about what it will bring, so I seek preparation for any potential outcome. May your power help me stand stable and strong." Not because I had lost faith in science but because I had begun to see its limits. Science can provide information on the transmission rate, model death projections, evaluate vaccine efficacy, and recommend public health measures. However, it cannot offer emotional support to grieving or comfort individuals experiencing illness-related distress.

Hebrews 10:24-25 [24] And let us consider how we may spur one another on toward love and good deeds, [25] not giving up meeting together, as some are in the habit of doing, but encouraging one another, and all the more as you see the Day approaching. This verse stresses the importance of meeting together as a community, encouraging one another in love and good deeds. Community is central to the Christian faith. From the early days of the church to today, believers have been called to live in fellowship with one another, supporting and encouraging each other in their walk with Christ. When I moved to St. Louis, Missouri, for a new role, transitioning from an infectious disease epidemiologist with the CDC Foundation to a federal appointment in the Research and Development Service of the U.S. Department of Veterans Affairs, my sense of community grew even more. My family in California has always been the cornerstone of my community, and ever since I migrated to the U.S., my church communities have continued to ground me. From St. Patrick Parish Church to the vibrant community at St. Francis Xavier College Church, I found strength and a sense of belonging.

John 13:35 says, "By this, everyone will know that you are my disciples if you love one another." This verse teaches that love for others is a defining characteristic of a Christian and a way to recognize Jesus' disciples, teaching that Christian love should be selfless, humble, and forgiving. For those with nothing left but hope, a community of believers can be a beacon of light in our darkest moments.

Romans 15:13 reminds us, May the God of hope fill you with all joy and peace in believing, so that you may abound in hope by the power of the Holy Spirit. As Christians, we are called vessels of this hope, offering encouragement and love to struggling people. Hope is a powerful gift we can give to others. Even when someone's circumstances seem dire, the assurance of God's presence and promises can sustain us. **Isaiah 40:31** says, But those who hope in the Lord will renew their strength. They will soar on wings like eagles; they will run and not grow weary; they will walk and not be faint. A. A loving community reminds the hopeless that God's strength is available to them, renewing their faith and resilience. Community support can take many forms, such as providing meals, offering transportation to medical appointments, or simply being present to listen and pray. These actions demonstrate that love is not just words but deeds, as emphasized in *1 Peter 4:10:* "*Each of you should use whatever gift you have received to serve others, as faithful stewards of God's grace in its various forms.*" Community is one of God's greatest gifts, especially in times of suffering and uncertainty—someone like me with stage 4 cancer, where the days ahead may seem few. The presence of a loving and supportive community can bring profound comfort, strength, and peace.

The community serves as a reflection of God's love and a reminder that no one walks alone. As I navigate the challenges of terminal illness, I find a community that bears their burdens through prayers, acts of kindness, and simply being present as a lifeline. This shared journey provided me with practical help and spiritual encouragement, assuring me that God and others deeply love me. Facing the reality of my limited time on earth, the importance of eternal hope becomes even clearer. A Christ-centered community reminds me of the promises of God that He is always near, even in suffering. **2 Corinthians 4:16**-18 offers this encouragement: Therefore, we do not lose heart. Though we are wasting away, yet inwardly we are being renewed daily. For our light and momentary troubles are achieving for us an eternal glory that far outweighs them all. A supportive community reinforces this hope, pointing patients like me toward the everlasting joy and peace in God's presence. My community helps me as a patient, experiencing God's love tangibly in my remaining time. Through shared moments of prayer, laughter, and care, I am reminded that we are not defined by our illness but by the love of God and the relationships he has blessed us with. **Psalm 34:18** says,

The Lord is close to the brokenhearted and saves those crushed in spirit. These words help me find solace, knowing that my community is a living expression of God's closeness. As a stage 4 cancer patient, the gift of community reveals that life, though finite, is meaningful and filled with opportunities to give and receive love. It reminds me that my life has left an eternal impact on this earth and the hearts of those who walked together. The community helps ease my pain and reflects the love and hope of Christ. As a terminally ill patient, I am embraced by God's grace and the warmth of my family. Beyond the academic world, I have found purpose in community. My faith community in St. Patrick Parish Church and St. Francis Xavier College Church has become my spiritual laboratory, where I experiment not with formulas but prayer, love, and humility. I attend services when I can, participate in virtual prayer circles, and offer reflections to others facing health challenges. We are all seeking something more profound. Together, we find it. I've understood that science builds bridges, but grace carries us across them.

Beyond The Timeline: Carried By Grace Through the Unknowns

While the unknowns are a significant part of the journey, understanding the knowns can provide a sense of control and direction. My Evolutionary Model can clarify cancer causality within the Unified Paradigm of Cancer Causation (UPCC). The Evolutionary Model provides a framework for understanding the progression and development of cancer. By examining the genetic, environmental, and lifestyle factors that contribute to cancer's evolution, we can identify patterns and connections that may lead to effective treatments. This comprehensive approach integrates various aspects of cancer causation into a single framework. It's a significant tool that considers the interplay between genetic predispositions, environmental exposures, and lifestyle choices, offering a holistic understanding of cancer development. This understanding empowers us, as it's not just about the disease, but about the factors that influence it, such as somatic gene mutation due to exposure to a known carcinogen, or UPCC, which sheds light on germline mutation inherited by kindreds at risk of other types of cancer.

When I was diagnosed with stage 4 non-small cell lung cancer, adenocarcinoma subtype with brain metastases, the shock was overwhelming. The news was heavy: a stage 4 non-small cell lung cancer diagnosis. Ironically, I spent much of my career researching this disease. As an epidemiologist, I studied disease patterns to improve health outcomes, never expecting to become part of this medical story. My oncologist said I had six months to a year, maybe longer, with treatment. As an epidemiologist, I knew the odds. The disease was aggressive, despite my MET exon 14 mutation offering hope for targeted therapy. The targeted MET inhibitor failed, and we switched to chemotherapy with pembrolizumab. Approaching the six-month mark, every scan felt like a final exam. Results showed stable disease: no new lesions and no observable treatment response. Upon commencing treatment for stage 4 non-small cell lung cancer, I transitioned from a theoretical observer to an active participant in clinical environments, chemotherapy infusion centers, and analyzing lab results identified with my name. As an epidemiologist, I had previously valued data, population trends, and the calculated risks inherent in public health decisions.

At this juncture, I was no longer merely a statistic; I had become a patient, experiencing fragility and vulnerability and hoping for continuity of life. This journey underscores the empowering role of communication with oncologists in treatment.

The first approach was chemotherapy, a key cancer treatment targeting rapidly dividing cells. However, it affected my kidney function after a few months, causing lab abnormalities, palpitations, and supraventricular tachycardia (SVT). Meanwhile, immunotherapy drugs assist the immune system in targeting cancer cells; however, due to adverse effects on my organs, chemotherapy was discontinued.

A pivotal moment in my treatment journey was when genomic testing identified a rare, targetable MET exon 14 skipping mutation. This discovery opened the door to a new treatment option: immunotherapy. This experience sparked my interest in Precision Oncology. Keytruda, a form of immunotherapy, could be tailored to my specific cancer type. This shift from conventional chemotherapy to a more precise treatment, thanks to molecular testing, was a significant turning point.

It also deepened my research interest in integrating molecular profiling into treatment pathways. The transformative power of precision medicine is not just a concept but a reality that offers new hope and possibilities in the fight against cancer. The hope that precision medicine brings is not just a glimmer but a beacon of light, inspiring us to keep pushing forward.

This transition was more than medical. It was symbolic of the evolution of oncology itself, from when every patient received the same regimen, to the present, in which biology and molecular signatures guide the course of treatment. It was also personal. As a scientist and patient, my dual identity allowed me to witness the promise of precision medicine not in theory, but in action. Immunotherapy had risks, such as the immune system attacking my body. However, the side effects were manageable, and its potential for a lasting response with minimal toxicity was better than other options. This chapter symbolizes the transformation in cancer care, driven by molecular biology to provide tailored solutions and new hope. In the space between progress and pain, I found purpose in surviving and observing medicine's advancements and the journey ahead. Hope is a powerful force in the healing process.

It resides in the quiet corners of our soul, often where we least expect it. Through suffering, I witnessed hope through white coats and genomes. Endurance carved character, and character birthed hope. This hope, when mingled with science, did not disappoint. Even in frailty, as God poured strength into my soul, I heard the splashes of every molecule in the language of his love. Communication with your oncologist is not just important; it's essential. It's a two-way street: you share your concerns, and they provide you with the best possible care, making you feel reassured and understood in your journey.

The best approach often combines treatments like chemotherapy with immunotherapy or targeted therapy, depending on cancer progression and body response. The choice between chemotherapy and Keytruda (pembrolizumab) depends on cancer type, stage, molecular profile, PD-L1 expression, and the patient's health. Below is a comparison of non-small cell lung cancer (NSCLC). Given increased creatine levels and chemo-induced palpitations, Keytruda (immunotherapy) is likely better for me than continued chemotherapy. It is not possible to definitively determine whether chemotherapy or immunotherapy with Keytruda is superior for stage 4 non-small cell lung cancer. The optimal treatment depends on individual factors, including:

- The specific type and characteristics of your lung cancer include factors like specific genetic mutations (like EGFR or ALK) and the level of PD-L1 expression in your tumor cells.

- Your overall health status: Your other medical conditions and tolerance for potential side effects play a crucial role. For instance, if you have pre-existing kidney issues, like I did, or if you are more susceptible to specific side effects, your oncologist may recommend a different treatment plan.

- Previous treatments you may have received.

- The goals of treatment: Is the aim to shrink the tumor, slow its growth, or improve survival? Depending on your specific situation, the goal of your treatment may vary. For some, the primary goal may be to shrink the tumor to a manageable size, while for others, the focus may be on slowing the cancer's progression or extending survival.

General comparison of chemotherapy and immunotherapy with Keytruda

Chemotherapy:

- **How it works:** Chemotherapy uses drugs to directly kill rapidly dividing cells in the body, including cancer cells.

- **Effectiveness:** It can effectively shrink tumors and control cancer growth in many types of lung cancer.

- **Side effects:** Chemotherapy often has significant side effects because it can damage healthy, fast-growing cells like hair follicles, the digestive system, and bone marrow. Common side effects include nausea, vomiting, fatigue, hair loss, increased risk of infection, and low blood counts.

- **Speed of response:** Chemotherapy often leads to a more immediate response regarding tumor shrinkage.

Immunotherapy (Keytruda): A unique approach to cancer treatment.

- **How it works**: Keytruda is a type of immunotherapy called a checkpoint inhibitor. It works by helping your immune system recognize and attack cancer cells. It blocks a «checkpoint» protein called PD-1 on immune cells, which can prevent them from killing cancer cells.

- **Effectiveness:** Keytruda has shown significant success in specific non-small cell lung cancer subsets, particularly those with high PD-L1 expression and without specific genetic mutations. For some patients, it can lead to longer-lasting responses compared to chemotherapy.

- **Side effects:** Immunotherapy side effects are different from chemotherapy. They occur when the stimulated immune system attacks healthy tissues and organs, leading to immune-related adverse events. These can include fatigue, rash, diarrhea, cough, and inflammation in various organs (lungs, liver, colon, thyroid, etc.). While sometimes less frequent than chemotherapy side effects, they can still be serious.

- **Speed of response:** Immunotherapy can take longer to show a reaction as it needs time to activate the immune system. However, the responses can be more durable.

In many cases of advanced non-small cell lung cancer, Keytruda is used in the following ways:

- **As a first-line treatment alone:** Patients whose tumors have high PD-L1 expression and do not have EGFR or ALK mutations.

- **In combination with chemotherapy:** For some patients with advanced non-squamous or squamous non-small cell lung cancer.

- **As maintenance therapy,** after initial treatment with chemotherapy.

- **After chemotherapy,** when cancer progresses, it is referred to as post-chemotherapy.

  Your oncologist will guide you in making the best treatment decision, considering your cancer's specific characteristics and your overall health. They will use biomarker testing results to determine the most effective treatment strategy. Having an open and detailed discussion with your oncologist about all your treatment options, including the potential benefits and risks, is crucial. This approach enables personalized and effective treatment plans tailored to individual circumstances. As my care team from Washington University and Barnes-Jewish Center selects the optimal treatment plan, please note: Guided by expertise through uncertainties, we can achieve clarity and purpose using my Evolutionary Model with the Unified Paradigm of Cancer Causality.

Throughout my life, healing meant diagnosing and fixing problems. As an epidemiologist, I studied illness spread, shaped public health strategies, and aimed for measurable results. Healing was about action and success. Afterward, I was the patient. Living past my prognosis has not been without cost. There are days of fatigue so deep I feel hollow. Some bring more questions than answers. But there is also clarity. I know what matters now. I know what I want to leave behind: not just my publications, but presence; not just findings, but faith. The irony is, as a researcher, the cancer I was diagnosed with, three of the papers that I co-wrote have been published since my diagnosis. Life with intention is fulfilling, regardless of its length. Grace has surpassed scientific expectations, and I am grateful for the unexpected blessings and unwavering support I've received. I face new medical tests and challenges daily, praying for stability, strength, and guidance. The Holy Spirit supports me through my treatments and doubts. Science and faith are now interconnected in my life. Grace is what steadied me in every given day as my body trembled. It is what gave me peace when my prognosis gave me none. Grace whispered to me in every roar of the MRI machine, reminding me that I am not alone. Even in fear, it allowed me to say, "God, I trust You." Through science, I discovered answers to extend life. Through grace, I found the courage to face death with dignity.

When the Lab Became My Sanctuary: Endurance Through Trials and Grace

In sterile laboratories and during quiet nights, I sought answers through science. However, wisdom is discovered and received through experience, beyond what any textbook can teach. "The LORD provides wisdom, knowledge, and understanding." - Proverbs 2:6. As I began to see the horizon more clearly than the road behind. It is not silence born of despair but the sacred hush of surrender, when the questions of science yield to the presence of something greater. I do not meet this moment with fear but with faith. Once my sanctuary of inquiry, the lab gives way to a sanctuary of light. Here, at the threshold of what is measurable and what is eternal,

In my first marriage, science provided purpose and structure when my personal life unraveled. Previously, as a clinician in general orthodontics, I did not have a license to practice dentistry in the U.S.

I was unsure where I belonged. However, distance, like time, can soften the edges of our memories. Life in the U.S. required new forms of strength, professional reinvention, personal heartbreak, and the unraveling and rebuilding of family. Throughout these challenges, God never left my side. My first wife returned to the Philippines with our two sons, Reighben and Duanne, while pregnant with our third child, Dwight. She did not want the life I was building in America, which was challenging and lonely as I pursued my calling. I remarried and welcomed my daughter, Abby. I became her biggest fan, just as my father had been for me. I cheered at her skating events, and her victories brought me joy I had never expected to feel again. Despite experiencing another divorce, custody disputes, and solitude, I continued. After my marriage concluded, I started afresh. Beyond heartaches, the voice of God and constant encouragement from my youngest brother, Rey, who was establishing his career as a Respiratory Therapist and raising a family in Manila, helped me move forward. Like many others, I was pulled across the ocean by circumstances I couldn't ignore. My father experienced a cerebrovascular accident. My future was no longer a plan; it became an act of survival.

While I was settling into life in America, my brother Rey, who was 8,500 miles away across the Pacific, received a terminal diagnosis of pancreatic cancer. His body was failing, but his mind remained sharp and his dreams remained intact. In our last conversation before he passed away, he asked me, "If something happened to me, would you go back to school?" It was not a command. It wasn't a burden. It was a sacred handoff—a dream passed from one brother to another, across oceans, sealed in love and pain. And I said yes. Yes, I would study. That promise led me to classrooms filled with younger minds and unfamiliar terminology. I was no longer the confident practitioner; I was the student again. I worked long hours, balancing school, work, and parenting. There were moments when I wanted to quit. Sometimes, I felt too old, tired, and lost. But the memory of my brother kept me moving. Each page turned, each assignment submitted, and each sleepless night was completed with the dedication to a goal. And in 2018, I walked across the graduation stage. I received a PhD in Applied Public Health Epidemiology. It wasn't just a personal milestone. It was a moment of completion. I kept my promise. My dissertation focused on pancreatic cancer, from which he passed away a year after diagnosis. The title of my dissertation is "Pathopoiesis Mechanism of Smoking and Shared Genes in Pancreatic Cancer." I wrote the following abstract for my dissertation: Pancreatic cancer (PC) remains a significant, unresolved medical issue due to its complex genetic blueprint and lack of reliable detection markers. This study aimed to examine the possible correlation between tobacco use, gender, and age in the etiopathogenesis of PC and other cancer types with a shared-gene association (CTSG-A). The unified paradigm of cancer causation was utilized to investigate the pathopoiesis mechanism of smoking and shared genes in pancreatic cancer (PC). A cross-sectional study was conducted using secondary data from the cancer survivorship module of the 2014 Behavioral Risk Factor Surveillance System survey. Ordinal logistic regression analyses revealed no correlation between smoking and prevalence of

PC and CTSG-A, but gender and age were significant predictors. Gender demonstrated a statistically significant effect on predicting PC/CTSG-A induction and promotion. The disease was more likely to develop at ages 62 and 69 years. These findings may contribute to a better understanding of environmental, genetic, and biodemographic interactions in disease evolution (induction, promotion, and expression periods). Findings may also be used to promote population health and improve health behaviors for individuals in vulnerable, high-risk groups. My commitment to a dying brother facilitated numerous opportunities.

It gave me language for what I had always cared about: equity, healing, and the health of entire populations. It gave me the tools to serve during a global pandemic. It gave me the credentials to speak up for those without a voice. But more than that, it gave me peace. To my brother, I have achieved this milestone. Your influence is reflected in my words, interactions with others, and efforts towards justice, compassion, and healing. If my parents and brother Rey had been here, they would have acknowledged my achievement of being recognized by Google. I spent much of my life in pursuit of evidence. As an epidemiologist, I am trained to ask difficult questions to observe disease, uncover patterns, decipher risk factors, and implement interventions that save lives. During the pandemic, this calling took on new urgency. Every data point on a screen was no longer abstract. It was a grandparent, child, or neighbor. Each hospital bed represented not just a clinical case, but a person with hopes, fears, and a story waiting to be understood. Through science, I sought to improve the quality of life for the sick, to find clarity amid chaos, and to stand between suffering and silence. During my initial years as a clinician specializing in general orthodontics in the Philippines, I observed firsthand the significant impact of access to care on patient outcomes. Later, in the United States, I carried that same fire into my work among marginalized populations, including the Navajo Nation, where COVID-19 struck with disproportionate ferocity. My work in public health became a bridge between science and justice. Precision public health, environmental data modeling, and risk communication were the tools I used to build that bridge. I believe that data can be beneficial when used with care. In November 2023,

I was diagnosed with stage 4 non-small cell lung cancer with brain metastases. I turned into the patient behind my research statistics. Suddenly, everything I had used to measure and understand illness became intimate, personal, and terrifying. The PET scans, biomarkers, and clinical trials became tangible and concrete rather than abstract concepts. They were my lifeline.

After my first craniotomy, I returned to writing and analyzing data with fierce determination. The second brain surgery tested my resilience in ways I never imagined. And now, preparing for a third, I recognize how fragile and sacred cognition truly is. What once came easily persistence. And still, I fight. Still, I write. Still, I believe. Because in that moment of personal vulnerability, something greater than science filled the room. Grace is what steadied me when my body trembled.

It is what gave me peace when my prognosis gave me none. Grace whispered to me in the silence of an MRI machine, reminding me that I am not alone. Even in fear, it allowed me to say, "God, I trust You." Through science, I discovered answers to extend life. Through grace, I found the courage to face death with dignity.

I wake up each morning uncertain about what the day will bring another scan, challenge, and fight to remain upright. Yet I greet each sunrise with a prayer: that God's strength would make me stable, His power makes me stand, and His wisdom guides every decision. The Holy Spirit has become my constant companion. He strengthens me when treatments weaken me. He centers me when doubt creeps in. I do not separate my science from my faith. I now believe the two are harmoniously interwoven. My journey with precision oncology proves that. When my genetic profile revealed a MET exon 14 skipping mutation, it opened the door to targeted treatment. This knowledge not only prolonged my life but also fundamentally altered its course. It bought me time to write this book, to witness more birthdays, and to finish one more manuscript. That is science. But the peace to accept whatever comes next? That is grace.

I continue contributing to cancer research, focusing on how individualized therapies can reduce toxicity, preserve dignity, and enhance life. My experience as a patient and practitioner has given me a rare lens that sees both the clinical data and the human cost. Targeted therapies, built on genomics and molecular diagnostics, are revolutionizing oncology. Yet their true power is not in statistical significance alone, but in how they honor the individuality of each patient. I am living proof of that truth. And so, I live each day as an epidemiologist and a believer. I draft research papers and support ongoing trials. But I also sing hymns during chemotherapy. I recite Scripture before surgery. I pray for healing, peace, presence, and the grace to let go if God calls me home. May my faith in the face of uncertainty inspire you in your journey.

The science of grace has taught me that healing isn't always about finding a cure. Sometimes, it's about finding peace in the waiting. It's about the joy of sharing one last meal with family, or the quiet strength to face another round of radiation. Healing is the assurance that my soul is anchored, regardless of what happens to my body. It's about writing these words with trembling hands, but a steadfast spirit. It's about believing that even in my decline, I am ascending. To every reader traversing a path of illness, doubt, or transition, I offer this: Let science seek the answers. But let grace guide your steps.

Through science, I sought answers. Through grace, I found peace. And through God, I am unafraid of what the future holds.

Purpose has a price. I learned this not in textbooks or journals, but in the quiet hours of separation, in the long spaces between phone calls from home. Letting go of the comfort of being near my children, my wife, and my culture. I exchanged the nearness of family for the nearness of calling. I accepted the trade, despite it being unfair. Before enrolling in graduate school and understanding the concept of public health, I worked as a dentist. I had built a life in the Philippines—married, raising my boys, surrounded by family. But then, during the pandemic, I held several roles in the Navajo Nation. As a COVID-19 Response Corps epidemiologist for the CDC Foundation, I co-led efforts with colleagues from Johns Hopkins University, the CDC, and the Indian Health Service of the Navajo Nation Community Mitigation.

I contributed to COVID-19 testing coordination, strain surveillance, vaccination tracking, analytics, public health, epidemiology, and safe school practices. I co-authored school safety reopening guidelines and initiated SARS-COV-2 genomic sequencing for Indian Health.

Maintaining the Labilles legacy has come with significant sacrifices, including missing birthdays and milestones, and the daily routines of fatherhood. The sense of responsibility has been a constant in every decision, serving as a reminder of the purpose behind these efforts: to secure a future and navigate a world affected by unpredictable disease and disparities in healthcare access. Afterward, I remarried and had a daughter, marking a new chapter. However, new beginnings do not erase past experiences. They build upon it, sometimes beautifully, sometimes painfully. The marriage ended, and with it came the gut-wrenching experience of a custody battle. In many ways, the courtroom felt like another kind of lab only instead of test results, it dealt with testimonies. It focused on uncertainties rather than facts. Through it all, I kept working. Epidemiology developed into an essential field of study. I found solace in patterns, probabilities, and logic's cold clarity. When personal matters became overwhelming, professional duties provided a refuge. It didn't numb the pain, but it framed it. I could ask questions with scientific precision, even if the answers were elusive. And yet, the more I sought to control, the more I was drawn back to grace. I saw it in my patients some of whom defied prognoses not because of new therapies, but because of sheer faith. Grace is not opposed to science it complements it. Science explains the "how." Grace sustains us through the "why." Together, they form a language I was beginning to understand.

Beyond the Horizon: Grace in the Last Light at the Edge of Science and Eternity

As time approaches, I feel a serene stillness, not born of despair but surrender. It is God's presence. Legacy is not just what is left behind; it is about preparing to return the contributions before me. I measure time by counting each morning as a new beginning, and being named after Ulysses S. Grant inspires me with his legacy as a steadfast leader during challenging times. While Grant's battlefields were literal fields of war, mine have been in clinics, laboratories, and hospital rooms. Despite the differences in our arenas, the essence of our struggles and leadership remains strikingly similar. Grant's courage and determination led him to the forefront of numerous battles, shaping American history, and then I helped in the deadliest global silent war. He faced physical warfare, commanding troops with unwavering resolve. Similarly, I found myself at the frontlines of a different battle against diseases and health crises, the pandemic. I fought tirelessly in clinics, laboratories, and hospital rooms to save lives and advance medical science. His legacy is a testament to courage, leadership, and resilience. Drawing parallels between his journey and mine, I find a profound connection transcending time and circumstance. His unwavering resolve and dignified approach to life's battles inspire me to lead with purpose and face my challenges with fortitude. As I navigate my final war, his legacy remains a beacon of strength, reminding me that authentic leadership is defined by the battles we fight and the grace with which we face them. Grant faced his final war with dignity, battling illness with the same resolve and clarity that defined his military career. In a poignant parallel, I am now facing my final war as a stage 4 cancer patient. I confront this challenge with dignity, purpose, and clarity, drawing strength from Grant's legacy. His example of facing adversity with grace continues to guide me.

I measure it in smiles from my children, in words I still remember, and in prayers whispered in the early light. Let it be said that I served.

I listened. That I wept. I pursued knowledge but held onto faith. That I walked the valley of cancer not alone, but with God at my side. I am not afraid of what comes next.

I believe that when my breath ends here, it begins again in eternity. That there is a room prepared for me. My parents and brother, Rey and Louie, are present and smiling. God will receive me, not for my degrees but for my heart. As I grow closer to the horizon of my life, I no longer ask how much time I have left I ask what I can still give. Legacy is not about grandeur. It is not built from titles or accolades, but from how we show up in moments that matter. It is in the lives I touched, the hope I kindled, and the light we leave behind for others to follow.

For much of my life, healing meant solving, finding the cause, fixing the problem, diagnosing, treating, and moving on. That mindset served me well in science. As an epidemiologist, I mapped the spread of illness, informed public health strategies, and sought measurable outcomes. Healing was about intervention, action, and success. Afterward, I was the patient.

When diagnosed with stage 4 non-small cell lung cancer with brain metastases at Barnes-Jewish Center, healing became about surrender rather than control. Despite this, my interest in science persisted. As an epidemiologist, my studies of health patterns couldn't prepare me for the personal battle with cancer.

This is a chronicle of my journey, the future of precision oncology, and the strength I found in grace. In the face of my diagnosis, I turned to what I knew: the potential of precision oncology. While I am undergoing treatment, I continue to test my cognitive abilities after two brain surgeries and focus on my current research in this field. Precision oncology uses advanced genomic sequencing to understand the mutations driving each person's cancer. It doesn't treat all tumors the same. It asks: What makes this tumor unique? And how do we target it? In my case, tumor profiling and extensive genomic sequencing revealed a MET exon 14 alteration a discovery that opened the door to targeted therapy. A therapy developed not through guesswork, but through decades of research. A treatment designed not just to prolong life, but to protect the quality of that life. This is the science to which I have dedicated my career. And now, it's saving me. Through precision oncology, I've seen how medicine can be tailored, not just to a disease, but to a person. The ability to predict how a treatment will work, what side effects may arise, and how best to manage them that's not just science. That's compassion in motion. Through the healing hands of my Washington University St. Louis and Barnes-Jewish Center care team, I am more than surviving.

It's being seen. It's being loved. When the oncologist first outlined my diagnosis, the words came slowly, deliberately, as if gentleness could soften gravity. Stage IV. Brain metastases. Targeted therapy. A prognosis of six months to a year. I nodded, absorbing each syllable like a calculation. Not because I wasn't afraid, but because, after a lifetime in science, I understood the language of mortality. But numbers are not destiny. They are tools meant to help us predict, not guarantee outcomes. I was expected to live no more than a year. But then six months passed. Then nine. Then one full year. And still, I breathed. Time, once assumed, is now treasured. Waking each morning feels like a reprieve, not a routine. Each walk I take, each meal I share, and each page I write is an act of defiance against despair. This resilience and defiance empower me, and I hope to inspire others in similar situations.

What does life beyond the timeline science has drawn for you mean? It means learning how to let go of fear without ignoring reality. It means celebrating the ordinary because nothing is genuinely ordinary when time is no longer promised. It means shifting from survival to significance. In the depths of despair, after receiving the diagnosis, I found myself grappling with the reality of my condition. The statistics were grim, and the prognosis was daunting.

Stage 4 cancer, often referred to as metastatic cancer, signifies that the disease has spread to distant parts of the body. It is a battle fought on many fronts physical, emotional, and spiritual. Living past my prognosis has not been without cost. There are days of fatigue so deep I feel hollow. Some scans bring more questions than answers. But there is also clarity. I know what matters now. I know what I want to leave behind: not just publications, but presence; not just findings, but faith. The irony is, as a researcher, the cancer I was diagnosed with, three of the papers that I co-wrote were published since my diagnosis in November 2023. I do not know how long I have. None of us does. But I know life is lived with intention, even if the numbers are whole. And I know that grace has carried me far beyond what science predicted. And for that, I am deeply grateful. As I was finishing this book, my neurosurgeon scheduled me for a right temporal biopsy and laser interstitial thermal therapy. What is a temporal Biopsy? This is a diagnostic procedure where a small tissue sample is taken from the right temporal region of the brain for analysis. It helps identify abnormalities such as tumors or other conditions. On the other hand, Laser Interstitial Thermal Therapy (LiTT) is a minimally invasive treatment that uses heat generated by lasers to destroy abnormal tissues, such as tumors or lesions.

It is guided by MRI to ensure precision and minimize damage to surrounding healthy tissues. LiTT is often used for conditions like epilepsy, brain tumors, or radiation necrosis. The procedure is expected to take place in the operating room at Barnes-Jewish Hospital.

As a scientist and epidemiologist, Grace has manifested in various ways. Even during the darkest times with unbearable pain and an uncertain future, I found strength not of my own making a testament to faith and a higher power's presence. My journey as an epidemiologist has always been rooted in pursuing knowledge and applying scientific principles. Yet, through the lens of faith, I have come to appreciate the harmony between science and grace. They are not opposing forces but complementary aspects of a holistic understanding of life and healing. The story of who I am is rooted not just in science and service, but in legacy in bloodlines passed through generations, shaped by history and grace. My surname, Labilles, is rare, almost mysterious in its appearance within the Filipino naming landscape. It stands out not just for its scarcity but for the questions it raises about origin, migration, and cultural fusion. Researching my roots has been both challenging and deeply personal. Labilles likely derives from Labille, a French surname from regions like Burgundy and Île de-France. It may stem from "la belle," meaning "the beautiful," or from geographic or occupational roots. Though I can't trace my family directly to Adélaïde Labille-Guiard, the famous 18th-century portrait artist, I bear a name linked to beauty, art, politics, and faith. This connection to my surname has added a personal dimension to my journey, reminding me of the beauty and resilience that can be found in the face of adversity.

As a scientist, the pursuit of knowledge and the application of rigorous methodologies have always been paramount. However, integrating my faith into my work has illuminated the profound intersection between empirical evidence and spiritual insight. In its many manifestations, Grace has provided a framework for understanding resilience and healing beyond the confines of data and statistics. In the complex field of epidemiology, where the focus is often on the spread and control of diseases, grace has been a guiding force, teaching me that healing is not merely a physical process but also an emotional and spiritual journey. Moments of grace, such as research breakthroughs or enduring adversity, have shown me that science and faith are intertwined.

The name Labilles reminds me that the essence of who we are is shaped by more than just our professional achievements. It is a legacy of perseverance, artistry, and faith, passed down through generations, shaping our identities and guiding our paths.

As I continue to navigate the challenges of my profession, I am constantly reminded of the beauty and strength that grace brings, enriching my understanding of life and its myriad complexities. I carry lessons from the past and hope for the future, embracing uncertainties that drive innovation. My legacy celebrates science, patience, heritage, and future aspirations. As I progress, I do so with gratitude and readiness to embrace new developments. The knowns and the unknowns will shape my legacy, and I approach them confidently. Each idea has shaped my scientific pursuits. Patience, a virtue cultivated through years of scientific exploration, sustains my spirit and allows me to face challenges calmly and resolve them. My heritage has given me a foundation to build my dreams. The past has taught me invaluable lessons through its myriad experiences, failures, and triumphs. Every setback is a step forward, every success shows what is possible. Heritage connects me to generations of wisdom, providing inspiration and strength.

While the future is shrouded in uncertainty, it is filled with endless possibilities. The thrill of innovation thrives in the unknown, and actual progress is made by embracing these uncertainties. My hope for the future is grounded in the belief that each new development, each novel discovery, has the potential to better humanity. This hope drives my curiosity and fuels my ambitions.

Uncertainties are inherent in the pursuit of knowledge and growth. They should be regarded as agents of innovation. Every unknown is a chance to broaden understanding. My legacy will be shaped by how I face these uncertainties, with confidence and an unwavering commitment to progress.

Faith has been my cornerstone, sustaining my spirit through the trials of scientific inquiry and personal growth. It provides a sense of purpose and direction, guiding me through the known and unknown. Heritage offers a foundation, a connection to the past that grounds my aspirations for the future. Faith and heritage create a resilient framework to build my dreams. Growth is not a destination, but a continuous journey, marked by constant learning and adaptation. Discovery leads to exploring new frontiers and unveiling possibilities. My life and battles are centered around this pursuit of growth and discovery, pushing the boundaries of what is known and venturing into the realms of the unknown. Embracing the uncertainties of the future is not a departure from my past but an expansion of it, enriching my journey and shaping my legacy. As I progress, I do so with gratitude for the lessons learned and readiness to embrace new developments. The interplay of the known and unknown will continue to shape my path, guiding my scientific pursuits and personal growth. With a foundation built on heritage and faith, I confidently embrace the future, ready to innovate, discover, and grow.

Readers have value and purpose. You are not alone. The light that assisted throughout each diagnosis, each page, and each breath will now guide beyond prognosis. Those reading these words may experience presence rather than absence. Let it be said in 2 Timothy 4:7-8: "I have fought the good fight, I have finished the race, I have kept the faith. A reward of righteousness awaits me, which will be given to me on that day along with all who have anticipated its arrival. I served, believed, and loved. I seek grace and peace with the Lord when science cannot solve a mystery.

The Core I Returned To: Where Roots Rise and Grace Remains

I built, I broke, I rose, I healed. But in the quiet end, a stage where I have found peace and acceptance, I saw what never left the enduring love and support of my parents, their teachings and values that have always been a part of me and guided me through life's challenges. Their love, a constant in my life, has been a source of warmth and comfort. My father's quiet strength, my mother's fierce, unspoken love. Their grace caught me each time I fell. Their legacy is remembered and persists and grows through every individual I encounter and with every breath I take. To the core of who I am, I return. And there, I find a profound sense of peace, a tranquility that soothes my soul, a calm that comes from embracing one's true self and roots.

Once scattered across continents and medical facilities, my life is now finding its way back to its core. I've realized this core was never a place; it was always the people. For me, that essence was firmly and unwaveringly held by my parents. I departed from home, saying goodbye to those who influenced my early identity, and followed their pursuits in new areas. And in those lands, I found what I was seeking.

When my father suffered his second stroke, I was in the United States, thousands of miles away. I had vowed to build a life that honored his sacrifice of love. But he never made it to the U.S., never witnessed the fruition of the dream we both spoke of in the quiet hours of ambition and hope. His death left an ache I could not bury, only carry. Years later, I returned to the Philippines after thirty years to say goodbye to my mother. Her lifeless body lay still and sacred, her face peaceful. I felt the full circle of life and death in that moment and remembered her unwavering love. My mother never needed grand gestures. Her affection was displayed through acts of care, such as preparing my favorite dishes, her anxious anticipation for updates, and her silent, continuous prayers for each of her children. She was the backbone of our family's faith, the quiet pillar of strength during times of scarcity and separation. Her love was not loud, but it was fierce. It did not need to be seen to be felt. In those final moments, I found solace in the memories that washed over me. Each memory served as a testament to enduring love, unwavering presence, and the grace of family ties.

The old had wisdom. It was the path carved by those who came before me: a lineage of hard work, sacrifice, and quiet contributions to humanity. My seeds of service were sown into my being long before I understood their purpose. Human experience includes accumulating knowledge, perseverance, heritage, and hope. Science shapes our thoughts and understanding, like the theory of relativity, enhancing our view of the universe. Scientific discoveries expand knowledge about diseases and other topics. Science guides and influences perceptions and the pursuit of knowledge. My legacy is dynamic, influenced by my experiences, aspirations, lessons from science, patience through trials, heritage, and dreams that drive me forward. Overview of My Journey, Identity, Resilience, and Consistent Support Life often clarifies rather than disrupts. Time progresses externally and internally, guiding us back to our core, to the initial caregivers who nurtured us, and the unwavering prayers that continually support us. I embarked on my journey with their aspirations close at heart, seeking approval in unfamiliar territories, such as academia and professional life, where their influence was not readily felt. The promise was made to my brother, Rey, about returning to school if something happened to him.

This promise became a driving force for self-betterment. Moreover, I pursued transformation following my diagnosis of stage 4 non-small cell lung cancer, adenocarcinoma subtype. As I approach the end of my journey, I realize that it is not the accolades that define my legacy but the quiet faith of my father and the enduring love of my mother. Their passion, a powerful force, has inspired and motivated me to grow and improve.

I found peace as I returned to the core of who I am. As I approach the final chapters of my life, I realize that accolades do not define my legacy, but rather the enduring love of my parents. Their love, the foundation of my being, is my true legacy. I carry forward their example and roots through my work, aiming to make a difference, honor their dreams, and help save the lives of the vulnerable.

My journey back to God through the science of grace is a testament to the power of faith and the transformative potential of integrating spiritual insight with scientific rigor. It is a journey that honors the legacy of my ancestors, embraces the mystery of my unique surname, and celebrates the harmonious relationship between science and grace. Reflecting on my heritage brings a profound connection to the past, grounding me in the rich history and traditions that have shaped my identity. My achievements, built on the foundation laid by those who came before me, are a testament to their sacrifices and wisdom. Heritage, a powerful force, is the compass that guides my values, providing a sense of belonging and continuity. It is the root of my aspirations, reminding me of the strength and resilience embedded in my lineage, and it connects me to a larger community, grounding me in a shared identity.

If you are reading this, it means the message has reached you. Whether you are facing illness, grieving a loss, caring for someone in pain, or searching for meaning, know that you are acknowledged. You are not forgotten. This book was written with an understanding of the present. Regardless of the results, may you find calmness. May you discover strength in acceptance. May your pursuit of science lead to curiosity. May you stay connected to grace. I've faced storms and surgeries, with trembling hands and a steady heart. As the end approaches, I don't fear the fading light. I've loved, lost, and served, kept promises to dying brothers, and walked paths lit by quiet prayers of parents long gone. I've made peace with time, illness, and unfinished pages. My breath slows, and I notice the stillness.   Held by grace, not strength, I'm ready to return to the One who shaped me. I'm returning to God's side, leaving this world in peace. As I acknowledge my heritage and review my achievements, I also consider the uncertainties ahead. This moment represents a transition that combines past accomplishments with future possibilities, where historical elements and new developments coexist harmoniously. "The righteous will be remembered forever; they will have no fear of bad news; their hearts are steadfast, trusting in the Lord." Psalm 112:6-7 (NIV)12:6 7

Epilogue

As I write these final lines, I am still here. Still breathing. Still bearing witness to a life that has stretched far beyond what I once feared, and deeper than I ever expected. Each morning, I acknowledge waking up not as a mere routine but as a privilege. A quiet occurrence, happening daily. The scientist in me still marvels at the body's complexity, the progress of precision medicine, and how a single mutation can shift the course of a life. But the man I have become sees something more something unseen. The grace that sustained me through surgeries, separations, losses, and the slow, persistent effort of healing. I no longer seek control. I seek presence. I no longer define success by impact alone but by integrity. And I believe that the most potent discoveries are not always made in laboratories, but in relationships, reflection, and surrender. Through our connections with others, we truly grow and understand ourselves. Through science, I sought answers. Through grace, I found peace. If these words have reached you, perhaps you, too, are searching for healing, direction, and the courage to begin again. I cannot offer all the answers. But I can deliver this truth: you are not alone even when the path is uncertain. Grace walks with you, too.

And as for me? I will continue to write. To speak. To breathe. Until I can no longer. And even then, I trust the story will go on.

I often think about what I will leave behind. Not the material things, those can be divided, sold, or forgotten. I think about the words. The voice. The principles that may guide my children after I am gone. In a world so loud with distraction and uncertainty, what could I give them that would still speak clearly when I can no longer? And so, I began to write. Letters.

My beloved Reighben, Duanne, Dwight, and Abby, If you're reading this one day when I am no longer here, let this be more than a goodbye;

it's my final goodnight kiss, one when the time stopped or at a distance when my words of love remain, no one could ever truly take away. I want you all to know first, and always, how much I love you. My love for you is a constant, enduring force, the joy of my life, the reason I kept fighting when the weight of illness and life felt heavy. I carry pain, not just from cancer, but from the broken places where life never gave us the chance to heal fully. Being a father in a divided home has been one of the deepest heartaches I've carried. I mourn the years we lost to silence.

I mourn the goodnight kisses I never gave, the birthday candles I missed, and the questions I couldn't answer when you needed me near. But I never stopped loving you all, not for a moment.

Reighben, my firstborn, you made me a father. The moment I first held you, my life changed forever. I was no longer living just for myself; I lived to guide, protect, and love without conditions. You've always carried a quiet strength, the kind I saw in my father. I hope you know how proud I am of you for becoming and going back to school again. Remember: You don't have to be perfect to lead. Just be honest. Keep showing up for those you love, and trust that God will walk with you even in your silence: Duanne, my thinker, my builder. You've always approached life like a chessboard studying it, moving with intention, never wasting a step. I see parts of myself in you: the observer, funny, the man trying to understand the world around you. I pray that you never forget to feel as deeply as you think. Let your heart guide your head sometimes. Let love be your greatest logic: Dwight, my youngest son, my fire.

You came into this world when everything around me felt like it was falling apart, but your spirit was light. You reminded me that God can still bring joy through brokenness. You made me laugh when I wanted to cry. You taught me to hold on, stay bold, and be kind. And always remember your father sees greatness in you, even when you can't yet see it in yourself. You've taught me as much as I've taught you, and for that, I am grateful.

Abby, my daughter. My grace. I was older when I had you. Wiser, perhaps. I am also more conscious of the time I will not have. You gave me something I never thought I'd feel again: wonder. In your skating, in your laughter, in your stubborn little heart, I found hope. I want you to know that you were never a burden. Not once. You were my miracle. I will always cheer for you, even when my voice is gone. I'll be the whisper in your conscience, the warmth in your triumphs, and the strength in your falls. I remember those freezing mornings on Lake Minnetonka. We skated like the wind, our laughter echoing over the snow, your tiny figure gliding beside me like poetry. Whether we were figure skating or rollerblading side by side, I was always proud. Not just of how gracefully you moved, but of how freely you loved me back. I am sorry, Dwight, that I never saw you make your first walk.

My love remained constant even when life separated us, courtrooms and calendars carved up our time. I prayed for you in every quiet moment. Deep down, I hoped you'd know that I never walked away. I was always with you, even from afar. If this is my final message, know this: Our pain does not define you. You are all the fruit of love, of dreams, of faith. You are my most significant legacy. And I want you to live fully, boldly, tenderly. I have hope for your future, and I know you will make the most of it. Love one another. Be kind to your mother. Be kind to yourselves. Forgive my failures. Acknowledge what we shared. Never stop searching for God's grace; it will find you, even in the darkest places. Though my body will rest, my spirit will be with you, every sunrise, every quiet night, every time your heart remembers that you were, and always will be, dearly loved. You provided support during difficult times. And in grace, I go peacefully. With all my love,

-Dad

What If?

What if from here, I am gone?

Did I get everything done?

Dying the first time, tired and depleted.

I tried, I fought, and in the struggle, I found peace.

Even when I'm gone, my memories will endure.

When memories fade, stories stop, then I'm done,

Dying the second time, expired, defeated.

With God, always, I'll be around.

What if my twilight has come?

Let go as dawn fades.

A life devoid of faith resembles the fading light of dawn.

Faith has fixed me; my life may be short, but I have not been cheated.

My hope and dreams, like stars in the night, forever shine.

What if I get wings shortly

As I fly, let the tulips sing

Acknowledgments

I offer my deepest thanks to those who have walked with me:

To my children, Reighben, Duanne, Dwight, and Abby. You are the light of my life. Every chapter in this book carries part of you. My hope, legacy, and love live in each of you. To my late brother Rey, your final request became my call. This PhD, this book, and this mission all started with your support. To the communities I served, especially the Navajo Nation, you showed me resilience shaped by culture, faith, and history. You changed the way I see healing.

To my spiritual homes, St. Patrick Parish and St. Francis Xavier College Church, your prayers, songs, and quiet strength gave me sanctuary.

To my colleagues in public health and my mentors in science, you helped me ask better questions and become humble enough to accept answers I couldn't find in the data.

To every doctor, nurse, and caregiver of Washington University St. Louis and Barnes-Jewish Center who walked with me in vulnerability, you became the hands of grace. Finally, to God, you gave me the courage to think deeply and the peace to let go. I began this journey through science, but I finished it in grace.

References & Selected Publications

Labilles, U. (2018). Pathopoiesis Mechanism of Smoking and Shared Genes in Pancreatic Cancer. Dissertation, PhD in Applied Public Health Epidemiology.

CDC Foundation COVID-19 Response Corps: Co-authored reopening guidance for safe school practices in the Navajo Nation. CDC Foundation COVID-19 Response Corps: Host, Long COVID Lecture Series. Unified Command Team, Navajo Nation: Co-led SARS-CoV-2 testing coordination, strain surveillance, and vaccination analytics.

Indian Health Service–Navajo Region: Launched genomic sequencing protocol during COVID-19 surges.

VA St. Louis: Host, Long COVID Lecture Series.

Labilles U. (2023). Comparative Effectiveness Research in Precision Oncology: Assessing the Potential of Individualized Cancer Treatment

About the Author

Dr. Ulysses Lagrimas Labilles, an epidemiologist, cancer researcher, and public health advocate, has a personal journey that has shaped his professional path. His academic achievements, including a PhD in Applied Public Health Epidemiology and the presidency of the Golden Key International Honour Society and other distinguished academic societies, are impressive. With a 3.8 GPA and a distinguished career during the COVID-19 pandemic and in precision oncology, Dr. Labilles has dedicated his life to improving outcomes for the vulnerable. However, it is his journey, following a diagnosis of stage 4 non-small cell lung cancer, that has led him to focus on healing, faith, and legacy, making his story one of resilience and hope.

The science he helped advance provided a framework for his treatment. His tumor profiling identified an MET exon 14 skipping mutation, allowing him to receive targeted therapy and personalized care. His journey included multiple brain surgeries and inspired him to write "Grace in the Genome," a memoir documenting his experiences. Dr. Labilles is the father of four children and has written about his medical journey.

www.ingramcontent.com/pod-product-compliance
Lightning Source LLC
Chambersburg PA
CBHW051245120626
46547CB00014B/1799